For my parents Lyn and Erich

**Many thanks to the staff and children at
Flamingo Montessori Day Nursery
and Teeny Boppers Nursery for their help and advice.**

Rainforest Animals

Illustrated by
PAUL HESS

Monkey

IF YOU WANT to catch a monkey
You're guaranteed to fail
Until you learn to leap from trees
While swinging by your tail.

Parrot

PURPLE, green, red, blue or yellow
The parrot is a colorful fellow
He sits at the top of a tropical tree
And loudly squawks – "Hey, look at me!"

Anteater

THE ANTEATER'S a nosy beast
With a sniffley, snuffley snoot;
He comes out at night for his evening feast,
A shuffling, whuffling brute.

Snake

DON'T ever make the bad mistake
of stepping on the sleeping snake
because his jaws
might be awake.

Jaguar

THE JAGUAR is wild – she's a jungle cat
With a frightfully loud sort of purr.
Her fine spotted coat
Gives her reason to gloat
And to spend the day licking her fur.

Toucan

WHATEVER one toucan can do
is sooner done by toucans two,
and three toucans (it's very true)
can do much more than two can do.

Tapir

THE TAPIR has no manners,
He picks food with his nose.
He swims and stomps the moonlit swamps,
With stubby little toes.

Tree Frog

"DEE DEEP," he says
  And stops, till when
  It's time to say
"Dee deep" again.